MEDALS FOR BRAVE MEN

MEDALS FOR

BRAVE MEN

by **NAOMI TALLEY**

Illustrated with photographs

 THE DIAL PRESS NEW YORK

To John and Valre

ACKNOWLEDGMENTS

My grateful appreciation to staff members of the Army Library, the Decorations and Awards Branch, and Army Publications, the Adjutant General's Office, for their generous help in furnishing material on awards used in this book. To the Office of Information, Department of the Army, for the photographs of awards.

To Mrs. John F. Davis for her research of old records and correspondence for material used in the Revolutionary War and Civil War periods.

To Dr. Richard Miller, Assistant Dean of the Foreign Service School, and Department of American History, Georgetown University, Washington, D. C., for invaluable information and reference material on the Revolutionary War period.

CONTENTS

1. Why Medals for Bravery?   7
2. The Purple Heart   11
3. Early American Medals—
        By Special Order of Congress   23
4. The Medal of Honor   33
5. The Distinguished Service Cross   42
        The Distinguished Service Medal   46
6. The Silver Star   50
        The Bronze Star   52
7. The Soldier's Medal   55
8. The Distinguished Flying Cross   59
        The Air Medal   61

1.

WHY MEDALS FOR BRAVERY?

MEDALS have been used since ancient times as a symbol of honor. When a man has performed an outstanding deed or service for his country, he is given a medal. The deed may be an act of great heroism on the battlefield, or it may be some other kind of unusual service to the country by a man who is not a soldier. So that the deed will be remembered, he is awarded a medal as a symbol of his honor and his country's appreciation.

In early times the Greeks used laurel leaves as a symbol of honor. The green leaves were made into a wreath. When a brave soldier returned from battle after performing deeds of great valor, he was crowned with a laurel wreath, which he wore proudly.

The laurel wreath was also given to men for outstanding achievement in athletics, oratory, literature, and civic work. A crown of laurel was the highest honor the Greeks could bestow.

The Romans, following the Greeks, also used the laurel as a symbol of honor. After a time the Romans took a more practical view of the award of honor. When a man had performed a deed of courage on the battlefield and was acclaimed as a great hero, they wanted something more lasting than a wreath of green leaves to give him.

So the Romans asked their coinmakers to create a design to be stamped on metal coins. There would be laurel leaves in the design, for laurel leaves were the symbol of honor. The hero's name and the date of his deed would also be inscribed on the coin.

The metal coins honoring a man for his accomplishments were a great success. Metal coins were something a man could keep. He could carry them in his money pouch. However, there was a disadvantage. A symbol of honor carried in a money pouch would not be seen. Men who had earned these symbols of honor wanted to wear them, as they had the laurel wreath.

Then a man, being practical, had a hole drilled in his coin of honor so that he could wear it on a ribbon around his neck. Soon a shining metal coin, hung from a ribbon around a man's neck, became a symbol that the man who wore it had performed a great deed.

Thus, from the early Greeks and Romans, the basic idea of medals as symbols of honor came down through the centuries. Many nations have medals to honor their heroes. The laurel wreath of the early Greeks appears on most of our own medals. The wreath of green leaves on the Medal of Honor, our Nation's highest award for heroism, is the laurel wreath, the first known symbol of honor.

The great Roman Empire fell and feudalism spread over Europe. Still the idea of awards for great deeds carried on. The strong men, or barons, held the land. They pledged the peasants to loyalty, to fight for them in battle. Whenever a man performed a great deed for heroism, he was given the highest honor the baron could bestow. This award was a title and the man was made a knight. The title of knight was coveted by all men. A knight was an aristocrat. Other awards were made to knights for lesser deeds. These might be a badge or a silk ribbon to be worn on a man's coat or his spearhead. It might be a piece of cloth bearing a design which pictured the deed he had performed.

As time passed, the knights' brave deeds increased. So did the pieces of cloth with the pictures telling of their bravery, and they were handed down proudly from father to son. The knights wanted these pictures put on banners so they could carry them into battle. To do this—to make designs for these banners—a business grew up called "heraldry." Artists took all the picture-symbols of a knight's great deeds and made them into a single design called a coat of arms. The idea spread and soon all the noble families of Europe had their own coats of arms. These coats of arms are a history in pictures of the deeds of honor performed in a knight's family.

After a time, awards were given only to those who were already knights. The peasants who followed them into battle and fought beside them on foot with no shielding armor were given no recognition for bravery. Nor did those who stayed at home to tend the fields and produce food for the fighting men have anything to show for their service. The peasants grew unhappy about the custom of honoring only the noblemen.

As feudalism died out, government by kings and sovereign state took its place. The fighting peasant retainers were replaced by national armies. Still, the old custom of decorations for aristocrats continued.

When Napoleon Bonaparte had himself crowned emperor, he was careful not to make the mistake the feudal barons had made. He had learned a lesson from their failure. Instead of awards for aristocrats only, he created a decoration that could be worn by anyone, whatever his rank or station. The men who wore this decoration were called his *Legion d'honneur*. It was the highest of many awards which he used to bolster the morale of his fighting men and, in turn, build up his empire.

Anyone could be a member of Napoleon's Legion of Honor. All that was required of a man was loyalty to the emperor and great bravery in battle. In creating this Legion of Honor, Napoleon showed his understanding that all men, whether rich or poor, aristocrat or peasant, could fight better if they were recognized for their bravery.

Decorations, later called medals, became a custom in many countries. In Russia the Cross of St. George was created; in Germany, the Iron Cross; and in England, the Victorian Cross. These were awards of honor made to men for bravery and loyalty to their country. It is from this background that our own medals—the Medal of Honor, the Distinguished Service Cross, and others—have developed.

2.

THE PURPLE HEART

★ ★

AMERICA'S first army was the Continental Army of the Revolutionary War with General George Washington as its Commander-in-Chief.

During this long war Washington saw a great need for some way to honor his soldiers. There were rewards for the officers, such as raises in rank or pay. For the enlisted man, who performed brave and often heroic service, there was nothing.

Washington visited his army camps and saw the soldiers suffering great hardships. They fought in bitter cold and in snow. There was not always enough food to satisfy their hunger. There was not enough warm clothing to keep out the cold, and many had no shelter.

The men kept fighting. The untrained, poorly clad soldiers seemed no match for the British troops in their fine red coats and leather boots. But they were and they kept on fighting.

Washington knew of the bravery and hardships of his men. He could not give them money, but he could and did give them honor. On August 7, 1782, he created the first two honors for America's fighting men. One of them was the Honorary Badge of Distinction, an award for faithful service consisting of a piece of cloth worn on the soldier's sleeve. The Honorary Badge of Distinction has been replaced by service stripes which show a man's length of service. The other was the Badge of Military Merit—the Purple Heart. Here is George Washington's General Order creating the decoration, the Purple Heart:

"The General, ever desirous to cherish a virtuous ambition in his soldiers, as well as to foster and encourage every species of military merit, directs that whenever singularly meritorious action is performed, the author of it shall be permitted to wear on his facings, over his left breast, the figure of a heart in purple cloth or silk, edged with narrow lace or binding. Not only instances of unusual gallantry, but those of extraordinary fidelity and essential service in any way shall meet with a due reward.

"The road to glory in a patriot army and a free country is thus opened to all. This order is to have retrospect to the earliest days of the war and is declared to be a permanent one."

The Purple Heart, the Badge of Military Merit, was America's first honor award for the enlisted soldier and the first military decoration. There had been no permanently established medals, even for officers. Officers received promotions in rank or raises in pay as honor awards.

Three men were awarded the decoration in 1783, Sergeant Elijah Churchill, Sergeant Daniel Brown, and Sergeant Daniel Bissell. It was on May 1, 1783, that General George Washington presented the first Purple Heart ever given to Sergeant Churchill.

How Sergeant Churchill won the first Purple Heart is really two stories. Each is the story of a raid against the British Army in the Revolutionary War in which Sergeant Churchill took part. The first was in November, 1780; the second, a year later.

Courtesy of the National Temple Hill Association

The first Purple Heart ever awarded. Presented by General George Washington to Sergeant Elijah Churchill in May, 1783.

Hayburners and Fort Takers

All day the men had waited, stiff and shivering from the cold. Hidden in a wood, they were waiting for nightfall when they would attack the British fort, two miles away. They dared not venture out in the daylight. There were too many British regulars and Loyalists about. The men were behind the British lines.

These men were fifty members of the Second Regiment Light Dragoons from Connecticut. They were used to cold and hunger and long marches. They were American soldiers fighting the British, and they wanted to end the long war.

Major Benjamin Tallmadge, who was head of General George Washington's secret service, had picked the men carefully. Word had come in from one of his spies of a great store of winter forage at Coram. More than three hundred tons of baled hay, enough to last the British all winter, was stored there. Coram was near Fort St. George. The fort must be captured and the hay destroyed.

When Major Tallmadge reported the matter to General Washington, he asked for permission to lead the attack. General Washington gave his permission. He left the details to the major.

Major Tallmadge had all the details. His spy had furnished them. The fort consisted of three blockhouses. These were connected with a stockade of twelve-foot poles, sharpened at the ends. Behind the stockade was a deep ditch and beyond the ditch was a high fence. Behind that was an abatis —a row of felled trees, piled closely together, their branches sharpened and pointed outward to stop an attacking party. They were as murderous as spears and bayonets.

Major Tallmadge knew that an attack on the fort would be difficult and dangerous and his men knew it, too. He had picked them for the job, and he knew they would not fail him.

To take the fort, Major Tallmadge must first take his men across Long Island Sound. It would have to be done in darkness by rowboat. On landing, his men would have to march several miles behind the British lines before they could attack the fort. It looked, on the face of it, impossible. But Major Tallmadge knew it could be done.

On November 13 he and his men set out for Fairfield, Connecticut. A violent winter storm swept down and made crossing the Sound impossible. They stayed at Fairfield eight days before they could leave. On November 21 the wind had calmed down somewhat. They would leave that night.

In the cold winter darkness the men rowed steadily against the rough water. They had left at 4 p.m. After four hours they landed on a strip of deserted beach, far from the point at which they meant to land. It meant a longer march to the fort.

By 3 a.m. the men were within two miles of the fort. It was too great a risk to march his men by day. So he ordered them to hide in the wood and wait for nightfall.

They had tried to hide the boats as best they could. If the boats were discovered, the men would be cut off from escape.

Tallmadge divided his men into three groups. He placed Sergeant Churchill in charge of one group of sixteen men. This group was to attack and take the largest and strongest blockhouse. Each group was to approach the fort from a different direction. Each was to attack a separate blockhouse.

Sergeant Churchill and his men were within fifty feet of the fort when the sentry shouted "Halt!" and fired. Almost instantly, there was a bedlam of shouts and musket fire. The entire fort swarmed with British soldiers.

Sergeant Churchill and his men went over the stockade and into the deep ditch. They scrambled over the fence and across the abatis as if it were not there. The British seemed confused at the attack which did not seem possible. Some stared as if in a dream. Sergeant Churchill's men took the blockhouse quickly.

The other two groups had not got over the barricades as easily and there were still two blockhouses to be taken. But the men battered down the doors, and within ten minutes all three blockhouses had surrendered.

Major Tallmadge sent the majority of his men to the boats with the British prisoners. With a handful of men, the major surprised the sentries at Coram and captured them easily. They pulled out the bales of hay and set them afire. There were two big fires going then, for the men left behind at Fort St. George had fired every blockhouse.

Taking a short cut across the woods, Major Tallmadge and his group caught up with the main force of the men and the British prisoners, who had not yet reached the boats.

By eleven o'clock on November 23 they were back in Fairfield. Since they had left, the fifty Light Dragoons from Connecticut had rowed twice across Long Island Sound, forty miles of rowing. They had marched miles behind the British lines. They had attacked and captured a fort, burned more than three hundred tons of British-held hay, and had taken many prisoners.

*   *   *

The second story about Sergeant Churchill is of another raid on a fort. Fort Slongo, a British fort, was on the north shore about forty-eight miles northeast of Brooklyn. The fort was a nuisance and General Washington sent Benjamin Tallmadge to look over the ground to see if it could be destroyed.

Major Tallmadge disguised himself as a civilian and slipped across Long Island Sound to Fort Slongo. Passing as a Loyalist, he stayed around the fort for several days until he knew every detail. He knew when the guards were changed and where every guard stood. He knew how many guns, cannons, and stores of ammunition there were. He asked the men what *our* chances were against the rebels.

General Washington had warned Major Tallmadge against the dangers of such trips. He urged him not to take chances. He was far too valuable to the service to risk such personal dangers.

When Tallmadge left the fort, he made a trip to Newport. He wanted to get help from the French Navy in an attack on Fort Slongo. But the French ships, based at Newport, were not there. They were scattered, some on a cruise, some elsewhere.

The matter was laid aside for six months. Then Major Tallmadge decided it was time to attack Fort Slongo. The fort would be a big loss to the British and a good prize for the Americans.

Tallmadge formed a company of one hundred men from the Second Continental Light Dragoons and the Fifth Connecticut Regiment. At 8 p.m. on October 2, 1781, the men started to row across Long Island Sound. By 3 a.m. on October 3, the fort was in their hands.

Fort Slongo was such a strong fort that Major Tallmadge had advised the men not to try to take it completely. Such a small party would not have a chance against the fort. They should only try to draw the British soldiers away, by pretending to retreat, then try to capture them. This would weaken the fort so that it could be captured at a later date when there were more men.

The men did not follow the advice. They attacked quickly, surprising the guards, and took it without any loss of their own men. The British had lost only four men when they surrendered.

Sergeant Churchill was in charge of the first attacking party. They took twenty-one British prisoners and destroyed a great quantity of food and clothing.

For these two acts of bravery and for strong leadership, Sergeant Elijah Churchill was awarded his Badge of Military

Merit—the first Purple Heart and America's first permanently established decoration ever awarded to an American soldier.

The original Purple Heart awarded to Sergeant Churchill is now owned by the National Temple Hill Association and is on indefinite loan to the West Point Museum.

*   *   *

The second Purple Heart awarded by General Washington was given to Sergeant Daniel Brown of the Second Connecticut Regiment of the Continental Army. Here is his story.

Victory at Yorktown

The chill of the autumn evening was penetrating on October 14, 1781, near Yorktown, Virginia, as the Second Connecticut Regiment made ready for action. The men had moved in so quietly that the British, protected by their redoubts, earthworks thrown up for protection, did not know they were there.

The Regiment was divided into two groups. Sergeant Daniel Brown headed one group. A young lieutenant colonel, Alexander Hamilton, had volunteered to lead the other charge.

Colonel Hamilton, with his French troops, would attack the inner redoubt. Sergeant Brown's group was to make the first charge against the outer redoubt nearest the river. The first charge is known to soldiers as the forlorn hope charge: they face the full strength of the first firing. Soldiers in a "forlorn hope" charge realize there is little chance they will survive it.

The order to charge was given. Sergeant Brown's men faced a heavy burst of firing from the British redoubt. But in spite of this the men forced their way over the redoubt. They did not wait to cut away the abatis, the sharpened tree branches laid along the top of the embankment. They moved rapidly in on the British, firing as they went.

The British were surprised and confused by the suddenness and the vigor of the attack. Within a few minutes, Sergeant Brown and his men had taken the redoubt and captured the British soldiers.

Sergeant Daniel Brown was awarded a Purple Heart for his victory at Yorktown.

*   *   *

The third Purple Heart awarded in the Revolutionary War was presented to Sergeant Daniel Bissell for valuable services. Here is the story of how Sergeant Bissell won his Purple Heart.

For Acting a Part

Sergeant Daniel Bissell did not take part in a raid against the British. His job was even more dangerous. He was a secret agent, a spy, for General George Washington. From August, 1781, to September, 1782, he lived as a British soldier in New York City.

General Washington had not been able to get important information he needed. His regular spies could not get through to the right sources. Sergeant Bissell was sent to New York to enlist in the British Army.

He got the information General Washington wanted but he could not get it out of New York City. He made careful notes of everything he saw or heard and kept it hidden for the time when he could get away and take the notes to the General.

His life was in danger every minute because the least mistake might expose him. If the British discovered he was an

American soldier, a spy, he would be shot or hung. But he kept on taking notes. He had to find a way out.

Orders went out that any soldier found with written information on him would be treated as a spy. Sergeant Bissell had to destroy all his precious notes. He could not risk discovery, so he memorized most of them.

After a year Sergeant Bissell was sent to the fort at Staten Island. At last he managed to escape. He made his way back to Washington's headquarters. There he wrote down many pages of notes from memory. He made a map of the fort at Staten Island and gave figures on the number of men, guns, and ammunition there.

For his valuable service and the information he had been able to furnish, General Washington awarded Sergeant Daniel Bissell a Purple Heart, the Badge of Military Merit.

Thus it was that three men were awarded the Purple Heart by General Washington in 1783. The records show no others. For almost 150 years the Purple Heart was not used.

But it was not forgotten. General Washington's order has said the award was a permanent one. When ways of honoring Washington on the 200th anniversary of his birth were being discussed, reviving the Purple Heart was suggested from several sources. It is not definite who made the initial suggestion. There were those in the War Department who believed the Purple Heart should be brought into use again, and they went to work to make this possible. There were months of discussion and planning. Three different artists submitted designs. Many letters went back and forth from the War Department to the officials around the country. This action was kept quiet until the proper time.

At last the work was finished. On February 22, 1932,

The Purple Heart as it is today.

the two hundredth anniversary of George Washington's birth, the Purple Heart was again an official military decoration. The War Department published this important order:

> "By order of the President of the United States, the Purple Heart, established by General George Washington at Newburgh, New York, August 7, 1782, is revived out of respect to his memory and military achievements."

George Washington's Purple Heart of cloth or silk, edged with lace, is no longer used. Since 1932 a beautiful bronze medal is given for the award. On the face of the medal, a purple enameled heart, is the head of George Washington. Above is his coat of arms between two sprays of green enamel leaves. On the back, under a bronze shield and leaves, is a bronze heart with the words, "For Military Merit."

Since 1933 the Purple Heart is awarded to soldiers wounded in action against the enemy. The wound must be serious enough to require medical treatment by a medical officer. When an officer or enlisted man is killed in action against the enemy or dies from wounds received in such action, the Purple Heart is forwarded to his next of kin.

In the many years when the Purple Heart was not used, other military decorations were created. For bravery in battle and other heroic deeds there are the Medal of Honor, the Distinguished Service Cross, the Silver Star, the Bronze Star, and the Distinguished Flying Cross. For fidelity and essential service there are the Distinguished Service Medal, the Air Medal, the Soldier's Medal, and other decorations and badges. When the nation was born in 1776 there were no medals, but special awards were ordered by Congress. The stories behind the brave deeds that necessitated these awards are filled with the exciting history of the birth of our country.

3.

EARLY AMERICAN MEDALS —
BY SPECIAL ORDER OF CONGRESS

WHEN the American colonies rebelled against British rule and declared their independence, they faced a long hard struggle. The American Revolution, begun in 1775, did not end until 1783.

Men were called from their fields and shops to fight against the skilled British soldiers. These untrained American soldiers fought bravely and endured great hardships. Many battles were fought and many lives were lost.

When the new nation was born, July 4, 1776, there were no medals for bravery. When the Continental Congress wanted to honor a man for a brave deed, a *special* medal was ordered and presented to him.

A gold medal was ordered by the Congress on March 24, 1776, and presented to General George Washington for driving the British out of Boston. Another gold medal was approved by the Congress on November 25, 1777. This medal was given to General Horatio Gates for his defeat of the British under General John Burgoyne at Saratoga.

A third medal was approved by the Congress on September 24, 1779. The medal was presented to Major Henry

Front view: (top) Made of solid gold, this medal was presented to General George Washington for driving the British out of Boston. The inscription reads "To George Washington, Supreme Leader and Preserver of Liberty."

Rear view: (bottom) Washington on Dorchester Heights overlooking the Boston Harbor.

(Lightfoot Harry) Lee for his attack on the British at Paulus Point, New Jersey, in July of that year. In the attack, Major Lee had taken 150 of the enemy with no loss of his own men. Major Henry Lee was the father of the Confederate General, Robert E. Lee.

The next three medals approved by the Congress were not given to officers. They were presented in 1780 to three volunteer militiamen for what was, perhaps, the most important act in American history. The men awarded the medals were John Paulding, Isaac Van Wart, and David Williams. The story of their deed and its sensational results cannot be matched for drama, suspense, treachery, and tragedy. It is the story of a British spy, an American traitor, and their treasonous plot which was almost successful.

Treason for Sale

On the morning of September 20, 1779, there was a touch of autumn in the air. The road east of the Hudson River above Tarrytown, New York, was deserted except for one rider.

The rider was glad that it was deserted. He did not want to see anyone. He had been told to watch for Loyalists—men who were loyal to the British king. He would have welcomed Loyalists. He wanted to see no more American soldiers.

Once during the night an American officer caught up with him and his guide. The officer rode along with them for several miles before he turned off. At the ferry an officer had stopped and questioned them. He looked at their pass and let them go. They had crossed the ferry and gone about six miles when some soldiers stopped them. One had seemed suspicious and had gone back to his tent and brought out a lantern. He held up the lantern and peered into their faces for several minutes. He held the paper close to the light and looked at it carefully. Then he told them they could go, but they must spend the night nearby. Loyalists had been seen on the road and it would not be safe in the darkness.

The rider, wearing civilian clothes, carried a pass from General Benedict Arnold. The paper read, "Pass Mr. John Anderson through the American lines." No one knew that he was not Mr. John Anderson but Major John André, an officer in the British army, nor that he carried secret papers describing an American fort to the British. If they found out, it would cost him his life.

Now his dangerous journey was almost finished, and he would soon be back within the British lines. His spirits lifted. He had just spent a night and a day behind the American lines. The night had been with General Benedict Arnold. They had talked until daybreak. Together they planned the surrender of West Point, the American fort on the Hudson River, to the British Army.

General Arnold had furnished a map of the fort, lists of guns, cannons, and ammunition stores, and figures on the number of soldiers, landings, and entrances. There was everything the British would need to take the fort.

John André had another reason to be pleased. He had saved the British money. For the surrender of the fort, Benedict Arnold had asked twenty thousand British pounds. André had promised him six thousand. After all, the Americans could never hope to defeat the British with their straggling army. They would be better off if the war would end. West Point in British hands would help end the war quickly.

André urged his horse on even faster. As his foot pressed the stirrup, he could feel the crisp paper folded inside his stocking. The paper was the map, the figures, all the secret information on West Point. West Point was as good as in British hands.

For more than a year Benedict Arnold had been plotting with John André for the betrayal of West Point. In the early years of the war Arnold had been a brave and daring soldier. He was a fearless leader and thought to be a great hero. He had been a wealthy man, and he was made a brigadier general. However, a bad leg wound inflicted in the battle of Quebec left him crippled and out of active field duty. He was accused of many dishonest business deals. He was censured by the Congress and court-martialed by the Army. He lost his money and many friends. He decided that selling secret information about the American Army to the British would be an easy way to win back his fortune. He made treason his business.

For more than a year Benedict Arnold had been sending secret letters to John André. The letters were in code, addressed to Mr. John Anderson and signed "Mr. Moore." They seemed to be ordinary business letters but each carried information about the American Army.

Benedict Arnold soon found that small bits of information did not bring him much money. He would have to sell them something big, something important. So he decided to sell West Point. Nothing could be more important than West Point.

Before Arnold could sell West Point to the British, he himself would have to command the fort. He wrote General Washington asking for the command, and after several letters from Arnold, begging for the post, General Washington named him commandant of West Point. Arnold took command August 3, 1779.

Benedict Arnold and John André finally met on the night of September 18, 1779. Arnold sent a rowboat under a flag of truce, with a guide, to the British sloop, the *Vulture,* which was moored just beyond the American line. The guide picked up Mr. John Anderson and brought him to the meeting place. He was to have been returned by the rowboat to the *Vulture* before daybreak.

The meeting place was a house overlooking the Hudson. Arnold and André had talked until daybreak when the guide rushed in to tell them the *Vulture* was being shelled. Up the river they could see spurts of flame and smoke of shells breaking around the sloop. As they watched, the *Vulture* sailed away.

There was nothing for André to do but wait until nightfall to leave. General Arnold left early for West Point, giving André two passes, one for water in case the *Vulture* returned, the other for land travel. At dusk the guide came, riding a horse and leading one for André. The *Vulture* had not returned, and André and his guide set out for the ferry on horseback.

As John André rode briskly along that September morning, he remembered clearly the nerve-racking events of the night. He had recognized the officer who rode along beside them. He knew his voice. André had kept silent and let the guide do the talking. Then came the stop at the ferry and the man with the lantern. André had wanted to finish the journey by night, but the officer said they must stay. The road was not safe because Loyalists had been seen that day.

They'd left at daybreak, and after a few miles the guide had turned back. There was no need for him to go further, he said. Mr. Anderson would have no trouble finding the way. It was only a few more miles to the British lines.

André was glad when the curious guide was gone. The dangers of his journey were over. He was in neutral territory now. No more American soldiers. Soon he would be with his own army, the British. He broke into song.

Suddenly his horse reared and almost threw him. Three ragged militiamen had stepped into the road ahead of him. One caught his bridle rein and shouted, "Halt!" André was certain they were Loyalists.

"I belong to your party, friends," he said. "I'm a British officer on business for the army."

The big man who held his bridle rein ordered him to dismount and show his pass. Suddenly André realized he had made a mistake. These were American soldiers. As André handed him the pass, he laughed. "I'll do anything to get along," he said. "I'm really a friend of General Benedict Arnold. I'm on an urgent errand for him. I must go along."

The men made him dismount and ordered him into a thicket to undress. The militiamen searched each item of André's clothing as he took it off. When he took off his stockings they found the paper. The big man whose name was John Paulding pored over it a long time. He could not read very well, but he could see it was something about West Point. "This man is a spy," he said.

Reproduced from the Collections of the Library of Congress

A Currier and Ives lithograph showing the capture of John André.

André offered to give them his gold watch and any amount of money if they would take him to the British lines. They would not.

They were ragged, dirty American militiamen, but they were patriots. They took André to an American outpost, North Castle, and turned him over to the colonel in command.

The colonel read the papers carefully. The handwriting on some of the papers was the same as that of the pass written by General Benedict Arnold for Mr. John Anderson. General Arnold had told him to expect a Mr. John Anderson and to pass him through the lines. Could it be possible that General Arnold was not the great hero some still thought him to be, but a traitor?

The colonel had a real problem. Should he pass John Anderson through, as General Arnold ordered, or should he hold him? The man might not be John Anderson. He could have stolen the papers and the pass.

The colonel sent a messenger with the papers to General Washington who would be at nearby Danbury for the night. He sent "John Anderson" with six foot soldiers to General Arnold. If the papers were stolen and the man was not John Anderson, the General would take care of him. The colonel also sent a letter to General Arnold saying that John Anderson had been taken with treasonous papers that he had sent to General Washington. The messenger with the papers about West Point left on horseback at noon. The soldier with the letter for Benedict Arnold left at nightfall on foot.

The messenger carrying the papers to General Washington did not find him. He returned to North Castle and gave the papers to the colonel. While he was away, a secret agent for Washington had come to North Castle. The agent looked over the papers and said it was a conspiracy. He wanted to go at once and seize Benedict Arnold, but the colonel would not agree. The colonel did send a messenger on a horse to stop the foot soldiers and return John Anderson to North Castle. He was also ordered to bring back the letter he had sent to Arnold. The men brought André back, but the soldier with the letter for Benedict Arnold could not be found.

Early the next morning, September 25, General Benedict Arnold was waiting at his home to receive General Washington and his party. They would have breakfast with him, then he would take General Washington on an inspection tour of West Point. His barge was waiting at the landing below.

Just as a messenger galloped up to the front of the house to say that General Washington's party was in sight, Benedict Arnold was called to the back. There a dusty foot soldier handed him a letter. Arnold opened and read the letter from the colonel saying that John Anderson had been taken "with papers of a dangerous tendency." Arnold ran upstairs and told his wife that all was lost. André had been taken. Leaving word with his aides that he was going ahead to await General Washington at the fort, he dashed out of the house. A horse was tied there and he leaped into the saddle and rode swiftly to the waiting barge. He ordered the men to row up the river to the *Vulture,* moored beyond the American shore. There he went aboard.

Back at Arnold's house, General Washington had been told that Arnold had gone on ahead and would receive him at West Point. At that moment, a messenger rode up and delivered the packet of treason papers to Washington. The General read the note, then looked over the papers. "He has betrayed us," he said in a shocked voice. "General Arnold has betrayed us." His men rushed out to stop Arnold but it was too late. Benedict Arnold had escaped.

Several attempts were made by the British to get John André released, but he was tried and convicted as a spy. He was executed October 2, 1779. After his escape, Benedict Arnold was made a brigadier general in the British Army. On December 21, 1781, he sailed with his family for England to make his home. He died at Battersea on June 24, 1801.

The three ragged militiamen, John Paulding, Isaac Van Wart, and David Williams, who captured John André and thus exposed Benedict Arnold's treason were given silver medals. Two of these medals are now in the New York Historical Society museum.

U.S. Signal Corps Photograph

The silver medal awarded to each of the three militiamen for the capture of John André. The above medal was presented to John Paulding and is on display at the New York Historical Society museum.

4.

THE MEDAL OF HONOR

THE Medal of Honor is the Nation's highest award for our fighting men. It is the most cherished honor.

The Medal of Honor is given to any member of the armed forces for an act of heroism in conflict with an enemy. It is not awarded except in time of war.

When possible, the Medal is awarded in Washington in an impressive ceremony. The President usually awards the Medal. He presents it "in the name of the Congress of the United States." For that reason, it is sometimes called the Congressional Medal.

The Medal of Honor was created in 1862, the second year of the Civil War. Men were fighting on the high seas, on mountains, in fields, and woods. Stories were told of heroic deeds. Men risked their lives to protect their flag. Some lost their lives in helping their wounded comrades.

There was no way to honor these men for their bravery. George Washington had set up a Badge of Merit during the Revolutionary War. He gave the Badge, a heart of purple cloth, to three soldiers in 1783 for their brave service, but it had not been used since.

A Certificate of Merit had been given to soldiers in the war with Mexico. This did not seem enough honor for the fighting men of the Civil War. They should have something better. People urged their Congressmen to give them an honor medal.

On December 21, 1861, a bill was introduced in the Senate to create a Medal of Honor for the Navy, and on February 17, 1862, another bill was introduced to establish a Medal of Honor for the Army. Both bills were passed by the Congress and signed by President Abraham Lincoln. Both bills became law July 12, 1862.

The designs for the first Medals of Honor were made in the Philadelphia Mint and were the same for the Army and the Navy, except for the way in which they were attached to the ribbon. The Navy Medal was attached by an anchor, suspended from a bar. The Army Medal was attached to its ribbon by an eagle, standing on crossed cannon and nine cannonballs. The ribbon had thirteen narrow red and white stripes.

The design for the Army Medal of Honor has been changed four times since 1862. There had been some objections to medals for soldiers in the beginning. Ribbons and medals were for European soldiers. American soldiers would not wear them, it was said. Instead, the Army Medal of Honor became too popular. It was copied and given away as prizes in contests and races.

There were so many imitations of the Medal of Honor that in 1904 a new design was made and patented. It is the design used now, and it cannot be copied.

The Army Medal of Honor is a five-pointed star within a wreath of laurel. The medal hangs from a bar on which are the words, "For Valor." On the bar stands an American eagle. In the center is a head of Minerva, the Roman symbol

The Army Medal of Honor as it is today.

of wisdom. Around the edge are the words, "The United States of America." On the back of the medal are engraved the winner's name, his rank, and organization. There are also the date and place of the event for which he is honored.

The ribbon for the Medal of Honor is light blue with thirteen white stars. This Medal is the only neck decoration awarded to our fighting men. The medal itself is worn only for formal military events. A small rosette, of the same white-starred ribbon, is worn, instead, on the uniform or jacket or coat.

Some privileges go with the Army Medal of Honor. Two dollars a month is added to the paycheck. The Medal of Honor was never intended to be a money award. That is the reason for the small amount. The Medal winner can ride free on military airplanes when there is space. At the age of sixty-five his name will be placed on the Medal of Honor Roll. He will receive, then, a pension of ten dollars a month for life. If he has a son, his son may receive an appointment to the Military Academy at West Point.

In the hundred years since its creation in 1862, 2,193 Medals of Honor have been awarded. Of these, 1200 were given to soldiers of the Civil War. Many of these Medals of Honor had been given to whole regiments, for taking part in battles. The soldiers who accompanied President Lincoln's body on the funeral train were given Medals of Honor. After the Civil War, regulations on the Medal of Honor were changed several times. All applications for the Medal of Honor were reviewed. Many of the acts for which Medals of Honor had been awarded did not meet the requirements. These were cancelled, and the names were removed from the records.

The first six Medals of Honor ever awarded were given to six men on March 23, 1863. The award was for an act of bravery that took place far from the battlefield. The act, one of great courage and daring, was one of the most exciting events of the Civil War.

To Steal a Train

The first six Medals of Honor awarded were given to men whose act of heroism was to steal a railroad train.

The train was the General. It had the biggest and best locomotive on the Atlantic & Western Railroad. This railroad ran from Atlanta, Georgia, to Chattanooga, Tennessee. The date of the deed was April 12, 1862, the second year of the Civil War. The men were Union soldiers.

The Union Army in Tennessee was trying to break through into the Confederacy. If the strong city of Chattanooga could be taken, the break-through would be easy. There was one way this could be done. This was to cut off the city's supplies, to stop trains from the South that brought supplies to Chattanooga.

General Ormsby Mitchel, head of the Union Army in Tennessee, called on a civilian spy to work out a plan. "Stop the trains from running," he said. "Do anything."

The man he asked to do the job was a secret agent, James J. Andrews. Andrews set to work on his plan. It took him several months. He rode back and forth on the road until he knew every stop, every bridge on the line.

The Western & Atlantic Railroad was Chattanooga's most important supply line. The General had the best locomotive. He would capture the General and take it to Chattanooga. On the way he would tear up tracks so trains could not run. He would tear down telegraph wires. No one would know until it was too late.

James Andrews called for men to help in a dangerous mission. Twenty-one enlisted soldiers volunteered. He did not tell them what they were to do. He only told them their work would be dangerous.

On the night of April 11, 1863, the twenty-one men boarded the train in eastern Tennessee. They were dressed in shabby civilian clothes and scattered in small groups through the train. They had bought tickets for Marietta, Georgia.

At Marietta they met James Andrews. He told them then of his plan. They were to board the General at 4 a.m. bound for Chattanooga. The train would make a breakfast stop at Big Shanty. When the train crew and passengers left the train, Andrews and his men would take over.

It worked out just as Andrews said. When the train stopped at Big Shanty, the conductor called, "Everybody out for breakfast." The crew and passengers went out on the right side. Andrews and his men dropped off on the left.

From then on, they worked fast. Two men ran back to uncouple the passenger cars, leaving three boxcars coupled to the locomotive and tender. Andrews and one man, his engineer, ran ahead to clear the switch. They raced back to the engine and climbed into the cab. The rest of the men had hidden themselves in a boxcar.

"Let's go," Andrews said. "Get out fast." The engineer opened up the throttle and the wheels started moving slowly. Suddenly, the big brass bell started clanging. Someone had forgotten to cut the bell cord. There were shouts in the station. "Open her up," Andrews said, looking back. "Get up some speed before they catch us."

When the crew in the station rushed out to the platform, they saw their big train, the General, speeding away down the track.

After they'd gone a few miles, Andrews stopped the train. His men tore up track and tore down telegraph wires. To make sure the track could not be repaired, they loaded the rails into a boxcar and took them along. There had been no telegraph connection at Big Shanty. No one would know. The men were jubilant.

Back at Big Shanty, things had happened. The General's conductor and firemen had darted off down the track on foot after their locomotive. They ran about two miles and came upon a track repair crew with a handcar. They took the handcar and two men. They pushed the handcar up the hills and jumped aboard and rode down. At the first station they found a switch engine which they took over. They set off again.

Miles ahead, the Mitchel Raiders, as Andrews' men came to be known, were sure they would not be followed. They stopped the General at one station and took on fifty crossties. They would be good to block the track, just in case of pursuit. At another station Andrews borrowed a train schedule. He had to know when and where to wait for "down" trains—those coming towards him.

At one station he had to wait for more than an hour for a down freight. Another freight was on the siding. The men recognized the General. They did not appear to believe the story Andrews told at every stop—that he was taking powder to the Confederates. Andrews sent word back to the men in the boxcar to be ready for anything. Finally, he was cleared. The General set off again.

Meanwhile, the Confederates were gaining on the Raiders. When they came to where the track had been torn up and the rails removed, they ripped out rails behind them and laid them down ahead. At the station where Andrews, with the General, had waited so long, they found he was only twenty minutes ahead.

At one bridge, Andrews had set a boxcar afire and left it burning. The Confederates pushed through the blinding smoke and nudged the boxcar off the bridge and onto a siding. They left it to burn. They had changed engines three times. One engine had to be run backwards to the next station where they found one headed the right way.

After ninety miles, the General failed. There had been no time for proper oiling, and the journals had burned out The Raiders leaped from the engine and fled into the woods.

U.S. Signal Corps Photograph

The General, on display today at the railroad station in Chattanooga, Tennessee.

Two days later the Raiders had all been captured. They were taken to Atlanta and placed in jail. Eight of them, including James J. Andrews, were hanged as spies.

In October the remaining fourteen Raiders broke jail and got away. Six were recaptured and taken back to prison. The next March these six men were exchanged for Confederate prisoners.

The six men made their way to Washington. There, on March 23, 1863, they were presented the first Medals of Honor ever to be awarded.

The first one was given to Jacob Parrott, not yet twenty, and the youngest man in the group. The other men to receive Medals of Honor were Robert Buffum, William Bensinger, Elihu Mason, William Pittinger, and William Reddick.

The other eight men who had escaped also received Medals of Honor at a later date in Washington.

The first two Medals of Honor awarded in World War I were given to two Marines fighting with the Army in France. One of these, Gunner Sergeant Fred W. Stockham, took off his own gas mask during a severe gas attack by the Germans. He put it on a soldier whose mask had been torn away. Sergeant Stockham worked on, helping to take out the wounded until he collapsed. He died from effects of the gas a few days later.

Sergeant Alvin C. York was called a "one-man army" in World War I. He captured 132 German soldiers, single-handedly, and marched them from behind their own lines to the American lines. He was awarded the Medal of Honor for this deed.

After the end of World War I, Medals of Honor were awarded to six unidentified allied soldiers who had died in the war. These soldiers represented the unknown dead of our country and our allies, Great Britain, Belgium, France, Romania and Italy. These men had sacrificed their lives in the fight for freedom—above and beyond the call of duty.

A Medal of Honor was awarded, by a special act of Congress, to Captain Charles A. Lindbergh. The award was made for Captain Lindbergh's nonstop flight from New York to Paris on May 27, 1927, the first across the Atlantic.

In World War II, General James H. (Jimmy) Doolittle was given a Medal of Honor for leading a squadron of bombers across Japan on April 18, 1942.

The story back of every Medal of Honor award is one of "conspicuous gallantry" and courage, above and beyond the call of duty.

5

THE DISTINGUISHED SERVICE CROSS
THE DISTINGUISHED SERVICE MEDAL

★★

THE Distinguished Service Cross is second only to the Medal of Honor as an award for heroism.

This award is made to any person, while serving in any capacity of the Army of the United States, who distinguishes himself by an act of extraordinary heroism in military operations against an armed enemy. The act must have been so notable, at the risk of life, so extraordinary as to set the soldier apart from his comrades.

The Distinguished Service Cross was created to take the place of the Certificate of Merit. The Certificate of Merit had been established in 1875 for soldiers in the Mexican War. At first the Certificate was given only to enlisted men, in honor of a brave deed. Later it was given, also, to noncommissioned officers, sergeants, and corporals, for bravery on the battlefield.

The Certificate of Merit was a printed document, signed by the President, and for almost sixty years there was no medal. In 1905 the Congress created a medal to be given with the Certificate. In 1918, during World War I, the Certificate of Merit was replaced by the Distinguished Service Cross.

The Distinguished Service Cross is bronze with an American eagle in the center. Below the eagle is a scroll with the

The Distinguished Service Cross

words, "For Valor." On the back is engraved the name of the winner and the date of the event. The ribbon for the medal is blue, edged with narrow bands of red and white.

The Battle of Midway

It was not the Fourth of July. It was the fourth of June, 1942, near the Midway Islands in the Pacific, and the biggest fireworks display in history was taking place. Midway was being bombed by the Japanese. More than a hundred miles away, Americans were bombing the Japanese fleet.

Long before dawn, at Midway, a message came in from a Navy patrol search plane. A large number of Japanese ships had been sighted about 150 miles distant. They were headed for Midway. Then another message. Many more ships, in several groups, were sighted. There were two cruisers, a battleship, many destroyers, and transports. All were bearing down on Midway.

Minutes later, in the darkness, a group of torpedo-bombers took off at Midway. They were to go out, locate the ships, and drop their torpedoes in a surprise attack.

At 5:30 a.m. a message came from another search plane: "Many enemy airplanes headed for Midway." About ninety-three miles distant from the Islands, 108 airplanes were coming in fast to drop bombs on Midway. By daybreak, every airplane on the Islands was in the air. The heavy bombers, too slow to fight, were told to keep out of the way.

Plane after plane rolled out on the runway and took off to meet the oncoming enemy planes. Soon the air was filled with the enemy fighters, Zekes, buzzing like angry hornets. From 17,000 feet enemy bombers dropped their loads on the Islands.

The first wave of bombers had come in at 6:30. By 6:50 a.m. it was all over. Nothing was left standing on the Islands. Everything above ground had been destroyed; only the airstrips were left. The enemy had saved them, expecting to take over later.

At the same time Midway was being bombed, the torpedo-bombers from Midway had located the enemy fleet. It was no surprise attack. The Japanese had seen them first and launched their fighter planes from the carriers. Most of the attacking torpedo-bombers were shot down before they could drop their bombs. They had flown out without fighter protection. The surviving bombers returned to Midway.

Of the land-based planes that had gone out to attack the enemy ships, there were four medium bombers (*B-26* type), the only Army Air Corps planes based on the island. This was the first torpedo-bombing attack ever carried out by the Army Air Corps. One of these did not return.

The next day, June 5, 1942, was a different story. Three Navy aircraft carriers arrived in the area. They sent attack after attack on the enemy ships. The attacks were timed so that the bombers reached the enemy carriers when all their planes were in for refueling. Four enemy carriers and their aircraft were destroyed. The victory of Midway was for our own fighting forces. It was the turning point for World War II in the Pacific.

On December 7, 1942, by direction of the President, the Army's second highest honor, the Distinguished Service Cross, was awarded to each member of the lost Army Air Corps bomber. The award was made for "extraordinary heroism." The men for whom the award was made were: Second Lieutenant William S. Watson, pilot, Illinois; Second Lieutenant Leonard H. Whittington, co-pilot; Second Lieutenant Gerald J.

Barnicle, bombardier and gunner, Massachusetts; Sergeant James J. Via, bombardier and gunner, Kansas; and William D. Hargis, Jr., Navigator, Oklahoma.

THE DISTINGUISHED SERVICE MEDAL

Many soldiers never carry or fire a gun. Many of them never see the battlefield. Yet their work is as important and as necessary as the fighter's.

In many of the jobs men must make difficult and quick decisions. On these decisions very important action depends. Some of these men have done important service for the government. Some service has been so valuable it has been rewarded with a Distinguished Service Medal.

The Distinguished Service Medal was created in 1918. It is awarded to any person in the Army who performs unusually valuable service to the country.

The medal is a beautiful one. On the face is the coat of arms of the United States. Around the edge is a band of dark blue. On this band are the words, "For Distinguished Service." Across the lower part of the medal is the date of the award.

On the back of the medal is the winner's name. There is a scroll, between flags and weapons. The ribbon has two outer stripes of red, a narrow stripe of blue, and a center stripe of white.

Here is the story of a winner of the Distinguished Service Medal. He saw a puzzling signal on his radar and promptly reported it to the officer on duty. What he saw were the bomber planes of the attack on Pearl Harbor, one of the most tragic and important events in American history.

The Distinguished Service Medal

Bombs Fall at Pearl Harbor

The morning of December 7, 1941, dawned mild and beautiful on Oahu, the Territory of Hawaii. It was a perfect Sunday morning. The sky was as blue as the sparkling Pacific below, with only an occasional puff of white cloud scattered here and there.

In placid Pearl Harbor the entire Pacific Fleet rode at anchor. Seven great battleships were moored south of Ford Island. Another was in dry dock. A hospital ship was nearby. There were nine powerful cruisers, twenty-eight destroyers, and five submarines. There were repair ships and supply ships, all the vessels necessary to service the great fleet. It was a beautiful sight on that quiet Sunday morning—one that would never be forgotten by those who saw it.

At 7 a.m. Staff Sergeant Joseph L. Lockard was getting ready to go off duty. Sergeant Lockard was a radar operator. He was in charge of the detector unit for the Signal Aircraft Warning Regiment of the United States Army.

Sergeant Lockard had remained on duty beyond his usual hours. He was instructing a new man in the operation of the aircraft-warning equipment. It was important work, a responsible job.

At 7:02 a.m. Sergeant Lockard noticed a signal on his radar that puzzled him. It was a group of specks. But the specks could be airplanes. That was strange, for no planes were out. The regular dawn patrol had gone out, as usual, but it had returned.

The sergeant checked again, very carefully. There was no question about it. Many airplanes, about 135 miles out, were approaching the Islands. Making a note of the exact reading—the distance and azimuth, or position on the compass of the formation, he went quickly to report to the officer on duty.

At 7:55 the Japanese bombers arrived. Within two hours the battleships were sunk or capsized. All the cruisers and destroyers were badly damaged. The Island base was a mass of ruins. Only fifty-two of the Navy's 202 airplanes could take to the air. All others were destroyed or severely damaged. More than three thousand officers and men were dead or missing. Three hours after Pearl Harbor was attacked, Japan declared war against the United States.

Sergeant Lockard's prompt action that morning, in reporting his radar signal, gave the Americans a little time. It was not enough, but some lives were saved because of it. For his valuable service in a position of great responsibility, Sergeant Lockard was awarded the Distinguished Service Medal.

6.

THE SILVER STAR
THE BRONZE STAR

THE Silver Star Medal was created by an Act of Congress, July 8, 1918, as an award for heroism.

The medal is awarded for valor or gallantry in action against an enemy of the United States in a situation which does not warrant the award of a Medal of Honor or Distinguished Service Cross. It ranks third in order in awards.

The medal is made of bronze in the shape of a star and is one and one-half inches across. In the center is a small raised silver star. On the back of the medal are the words, "For Gallantry in Action." The medal is attached to its ribbon by a metal loop. The ribbon has a center stripe of red, a stripe of white, a stripe of blue, a narrow white, and a narrow blue stripe.

A Silver Star for Christmas

The Silver Star Medal awarded to Private First Class Thomas J. McNamara was really a Star for Christmas.

On Christmas Day, 1944, Private McNamara was fighting with the infantry in Belgium. It was in World War II and the great Battle of the Bulge was on. Our Army was fighting hard to push the German troops back.

The Silver Star Medal

The Germans had made a strong attack. Private McNamara's company was under heavy fire, for the enemy had surrounded his command post. They had cut his company off from an important forward position. Some noncommissioned officers and men had been wounded and could not carry on.

With no regard for his own safety, Private McNamara went out in front of his lines. He was in full view of the enemy and exposed to their heavy fire. But he had decided if he could see the enemy gun positions, he could tell his own mortar gun crews where to direct their fire.

Private McNamara stayed out in front for two hours. With the information he gave his own gunners, they disabled the enemy guns and put them out of action. When the firing stopped, Private McNamara took the enemy gun crews prisoners. He had them carry his wounded men to a place of safety. Then he delivered his prisoners to the officer in charge.

Private McNamara was awarded a Silver Star for his bravery in the face of danger. The Christmas of 1944 was one he would remember.

THE BRONZE STAR

The Bronze Star Medal, created on February 4, 1944, is also an award for heroism in conflict with an enemy of the United States. It is given for bravery in a situation of lesser importance or in which there is a lesser degree of danger than that of the Silver Star. It is often awarded for meritorious service which, while in connection with combat, has not been performed in actual combat.

This medal can be awarded to any person in the Army, the Navy, or the Marine Corps for heroic action. The action to earn the medal must have been after December 7, 1941.

The medal is a bronze star with a small bronze star in the center. On the back of it are the words, "Heroic or Meritorious Action." There is also the name of the person who receives the award.

The medal is attached to its ribbon by a metal loop. The ribbon is Old Glory red, with a center stripe of royal blue edged with white. The outer edge of the ribbon is white.

U.S. Army Photograph

The Bronze Star Medal

Here is a story of how one brave soldier won a Bronze Star Medal.

He Kept the Channels Open

Was that any way to fight a war? To operate a radio or repair telephone lines? Technician Fourth Class Robert L. Gorny found out that it was a very important way to fight a war. Radios and telephones were very necessary. All sorts of messages went over them. There was information about enemy movements, battles were ordered—everything in code, of course. And, like the mail, the messages must go through.

Technician Gorny was with an armored division in Europe in World War II. If he wanted action, he had found it. From January to May, 1945, his division was in the Battle of the Ardennes, the break-through of the Siegfried Lines, the drive on the Rhine River, the clearing of the Moselle-Rhine River triangle, and the hard push into Germany and Austria.

Technician Gorny was a radio operator. If a radio blanked out, he had to get it operating again fast. If a telephone line failed, he had to find the trouble and repair it.

He worked in all kinds of weather—rain, sleet, or snow. He worked under heavy enemy fire. He could not wait until the enemy shells stopped coming over. They didn't stop. A man on a telephone pole was a good enemy target. Some of the crew found that out. While they were out of service, Technician Gorny carried on, doing their work as well as his own.

Many times Technician Gorny worked around the clock with no sleep and little food. The channels must be kept open. Messages must go through.

Technician Gorny's untiring work under enemy fire was a very important part in fighting a winning war. For his unselfish heroic service, he was awarded the Bronze Star Medal.

7.

THE SOLDIER'S MEDAL

★★★★★★★★★★★★★★★★★★★★★★★★★★★★★★★★★★★★★

NOT all acts of heroism take place on the battlefield. Not all are in conflict with the enemy. Many a soldier has faced dangerous situations when only by quick thinking and courageous action can another's life be saved. He does so at the risk of his own life. It is such courage that makes a man a hero.

There is an award for such heroism. It is the Soldier's Medal. Created in July, 1926, the Soldier's Medal is awarded to anyone in the armed forces for an act of heroism not in conflict with the enemy. It may be given also to men from friendly foreign nations while serving with our army.

The Soldier's Medal is an octagon of bronze, one and one-half inches across. In the center is an eagle standing between two groups of stars. On the back is the shield of the United States, and on each side of the shield is a spray of oak and laurel leaves. Around the edge, at the top, are the words, "Soldier's Medal." Across the lower half are the words, "For Valor." The ribbon for the medal has two outer bands of blue. In the center are thirteen narrow stripes of red and white.

Almost every Soldier's Medal awarded means that one

The Soldier's Medal

or more lives have been saved at the risk of a soldier's life. One member of the Women's Army Corps, at West Hampton Beach, New York, swam two hundred yards through rough water and high waves to save a fellow WAC from drowning. Two others had tried and failed.

Here is the story of a soldier who risked great danger at night to save the lives of four men.

Trapped in a Mine Field

October 13, 1951, was truly an unlucky day for four American soldiers in Korea. They were trapped in a mine field, near the village of Moyre Dong. Before they realized their danger, they were in a cluster of mines. One mine exploded and three of the men were severely wounded.

The men had been out on a night patrol mission and were returning to their base when the mine explosion caught them. The only man not injured was able to get a radio message through to the base. Three of the men needed medical attention as quickly as possible.

When the word came in that the men were trapped, Second Lieutenant David R. Bauer volunteered immediately for the rescue operation. Everyone knew that it was dangerous. Lieutenant Bauer knew it. But the men were trapped. They had to be brought out. He would do it.

Very quickly, Lieutenant Bauer got together the probing and marking material. This was needed to locate the mines and mark a safe path through to the men for their return. He called for medical aid and lights needed for treating the wounded men. In a very short time Lieutenant Bauer was on his way with his helpers to the area where the men were trapped.

He left his helpers at a safe distance from the mined area, then went on alone. He worked quickly in the pitch-black darkness in an effort to reach the trapped men.

The ground of the mine field was covered with a thick tangle of matted vines. Lieutenant Bauer had to probe cautiously every few inches before he could take a step forward. In spite of the darkness and the danger of exploding mines, he worked quickly through seventy-five feet of mine field. The mines were the antipersonnel type. The pressure of a man's foot would explode them.

When he reached the men, Lieutenant Bauer found that two of them had died from their wounds. Helping the wounded man, the uninjured one following, he led the way back through the narrow zigzag path he had marked.

Lieutenant Bauer made two trips back along the dangerous path to bring out the two soldiers who had died from their wounds. Each trip was made in the face of grave danger. A step only a few inches too far to the right or left could set off a mine.

Second Lieutenant Bauer saved the lives at the risk of his own. For this courageous act he was awarded the Soldier's Medal, For Valor.

8

THE DISTINGUISHED FLYING CROSS
THE AIR MEDAL

MANY deeds of great courage take place in air battles with the enemy. Every air attack, every bombing raid is made possible by the brave men who fly the planes.

There are, too, men in aircraft who risk their lives in the face of great danger away from the battlefield. Even in time of peace some men have faced dangerous situations, where only by quick thinking and action, a tragedy was prevented.

On July 2, 1926, the Congress passed an act to create the Distinguished Flying Cross. The medal is given to any member of the armed forces who performs with exceptional heroism while making a flight in an Army aircraft. This applied only to flights taking place after April 19, 1917.

The Distinguished Flying Cross is a bronze medal. A four-bladed propeller is set against a Maltese cross, filled in with fluted bronze. The medal hangs from a ribbon with vertical stripes in this order: blue, white, blue, white, red, white, blue, white, blue.

The Distinguished Flying Cross

Rescue Flights Over Flood Waters

Captain James R. Sulpizi is a U. S. Army captain assigned to duty with the Delaware Coast Guard. Captain Sulpizi was awarded a Distinguished Flying Cross for his heroic rescue work on the night of March 7, 1962.

On that night a disastrous storm, with high winds and rains, struck the coast of Delaware. At Indian River flood waters rushed in and many people, clinging to treetops and floating debris, were in danger of drowning. The winds were of such gale force that all air flights would be cancelled. Captain Sulpizi volunteered to fly the only aircraft at hand, a small one-passenger *H-13* helicopter, to rescue the persons in danger of drowning from the high flood waters.

The strong winds made flying the helicopter a dangerous operation, but Captain Sulpizi made trip after trip, each time bringing a person to safety. The trips were nine miles each way. Ten times he made the round trip. He rescued five persons from the Coast Guard Station, then searched and found five others clinging to trucks that were afloat on the surging waters. Through the wind and the torrents of rain he worked doggedly, each trip saving a life and each trip risking his own.

Captain Sulpizi did not end his rescue flights until a large helicopter flew in to take over the work. Captain Sulpizi was awarded a Distinguished Flying Cross for his brave and heroic action in saving ten lives.

THE AIR MEDAL

The Air Medal was established by the President in 1942. This medal may be awarded to anyone for valuable service in

The Air Medal

flight while serving in the Army. The award is made for such acts only after September 9, 1939. The medal may also be awarded to civilians.

The Air Medal is a compass of bronze. On the face of the compass is a bronze disc. Across this disc is an eagle in flight carrying two flashes of lightning in its claws.

The ribbon for the medal is Marine blue with two outer stripes of orange, edged with white.

Many Air Medals were awarded for service to our country in World War II. Most of these flights were made under highly dangerous conditions. They were acts of courage and unselfish service.

One civilian from the Office of War Information made twenty-five flights from September 1 to November 20, 1944. The flights were over rugged mountains in Japan and Burma. The purpose was to drop information leaflets to Japanese soldiers and the people in enemy-held Burma. The flights were without fighter escort and subject to enemy fire. They were acts of courage and unselfish service. This was one of many services for which Air Medals were awarded.

The history of medals follows the history of America. These stories are about only a few of the men who have been awarded medals—not necessarily the bravest men, for they were all brave. There are heroic men in all the services—the Army, the Air Force, the Navy, and the Marine Corps—but all their stories would fill many books.

When George Washington created America's first military decoration, the Purple Heart, he said, "The road to glory in a patriot army and a free country is thus open to all."

These men, in the stories in this book, found the road to glory.

NAOMI TALLEY

lives in Washington, D. C., where she worked for many years as both a writer and editor for Army Publications, the Department of the Army. Born in Texas, Mrs. Talley was formerly a teacher in the elementary grades in Fort Worth. Her poems, short stories, and articles have appeared in many magazines, and her first book, *Imported Insects,* was published in 1961.

355.1
Tal   **Talley, Naomi**
      Medals for brave men

4025

Brief notes on medals given to Americans
for acts of bravery, from Purple Heart to
Air Medal.

Blairsville Junior High School
Blairsville, Pennsylvania